The Search For Solace

Orangebooks Publication

Smriti Nagar, Bhilai, Chhattisgarh - 490020

Website: **www.orangebooks.in**

© Copyright, 2023, Author

All rights reserved. No part of this book may be reproduced, stored in a retrieval system, or transmitted, in any form by any means, electronic, mechanical, magnetic, optical, chemical, manual, photocopying, recording or otherwise, without the prior written consent of its writer.

THE SEARCH FOR SOLACE

A Sail Through The Tides Of Teenage

SUHANI CHADHA

OrangeBooks Publication
www.orangebooks.in

About Book

The Search For Solace, takes you on a journey that brings to you a taste of the sweet and sour of teenage, the varying experiences that this golden phase of life has to offer. It's an attempt to bring forward the truths, plights and delights that teen years bring up, and the vital lessons of life these times bless a soul with.

About Author

Suhani Chadha is a 16 year old aspiring young author, who is passionate about creating an impact through her inspiring words. She writes for the pure joy of the thing, transforming words into an impressive source of magic. She wishes to bring significant chnages in the outlook of the society, transforming it into an ideal and inspiring one, through her writings.

INDEX

A Mystery Called Life…................................. 1

Loads Of Happiness To Myself…..................... 3

A Lot More Fights, Changes, And Emotions…............. 5

It Might Not Always Work Well…................ 7

I'm Still Writing… 9

It Could Be… 11

Is It The World Or The Way I Look ?........................... 13

It Just Happened, Am Glad It Did… 15

We Talked Today… 17

Am I Still Lost ? 19

Those Sweet Bonds… 21

The Guide To Growing Up…....................... 23

Shatterings Yet Power… 25

A Closer Look At This Face…...................... 26

Too Many Expectations…............................ 28

Lost Dreams And Hopes To Shine…............................ 30

The Reel Real Game…................................. 32

Maybe She's Better ! Well, I Accept…......................... 34

The Urge To Say Out The Word… 36

When I've Got No Helping Hands…............................. 38

She's Been There For Me Always…............................ 40

Music Does It All For Me… 42

The Two Of You Have Been The
Spark From Within… 44

It's You, My Teacher… 46

I Too Wish… 47

Finding Newer Reasons To Stay Happy…..................... 49

Life's Got Newer People Waiting For You… 51

My Expression Of Experiences And Emotions…......... 53

That's How You Live Through… 55

A Look Back At The Year…... 57

A Mystery Called Life...

Life's an ever evolving puzzle, a cluster of undying emotions, and a journey encompassing mysteries and challenges. But the ultimate destination of this mystery called life is the attainment of eternal peace and satisfaction.

I close my eyes and I can see,
A world that's waiting up for me.
My mind's filled with new thoughts,
A whole lot of varying sorts.
Some bless this empty soul with an elixir of delight,
While others throw upon a helpless plight.
Stories come up, events formulate,
Either exciting the mind or worsening the state.
But as soon as these eyes open up to see the world around,
There're millions of those bees making the buzzing sound.
The sound that inspires, or the one that annoys,
It's up to us to choose whether to sink or sail through canoes.
It's up to us, the way we perceive this buzzing,
For this is life and it never stops puzzling.
Sailing through these seas of hardships is all that matters,
These challenges test our human abilities, our passion is all it caters.

Love, fame and money are all feathers to this cap,
So called life, you've got to make up your own map.
Running after these feathers shall steal the precious pot of time,
You might turn up selfish, forgetting the dreams to shine.
Learn to live in the moment, enjoy the present,
For who's seen the future, on what it's to depend.
Look up around and you'll find tons to inspire,
Means to grow and learn, a new lot of desires.
Desires to find the true self, to learn the art of loving self,
Desires to discover the ultimate truth, for life's a mystery in itself.

Loads Of Happiness To Myself...

Got tasks to do, I'm still awake,

Working towards the accomplishment of the goals I make.

I've become quite different, an entirely changed person now,

Trynna balance it all and learn the knowhow.

Soon I come face to face with some of the unexpected truths,

Something that seems quite strange, doesn't fit in and never seems to suit.

This is how I feel exactly right now,

Am trying to figure out the causes for some decisions, tracing the hows.

I've got a mix of feelings,

Some past pains that've been revived or some long lost healings.

Am treading a path, the destination however is unknown,

What's coming up are just the consequences of what I've sown.

I'm totally unaware of what this journey has in store for me,

Some chances to be the happiest soul on Earth or some obstructions I can't see.

I'm for sure not sad, not even depressed,

Just some nervousness with a pinch of stress.

That's making me doubt my abilities,

Causing me to turn a blind eye to quite a few opportunities.

I'm still struggling to learn the art of seeing the good in every situation,

Even a refusal from someone or an unexpected condition,

Can transform my good day mood into a totally different one,

Causing this satisfied soul to see no more good and happiness in anyone.

I can't name this sort of emotion,

It causes a bit of stress and a whole lot of tension.

That's why I'm here writing, sharing it with you,

Making an effort to get it all off my chest, directing to the start of something new.

Am desirous of a new pleasant day,

Filled with laughter and fun, a thread of joy and positive ray.

At night however, I'm always the same,

Going through this similar emptiness and an emotion that I can't still name.

Penning it all down, soon calms me to some extent,

Loads of joy, happiness and love to myself, is what I intend to send.

A Lot More Fights, Changes, And Emotions...

Everyone's asleep, but I'm still awake,
Preparing for the Exam the next day, success for myself is what I wish to make.
I wish to sleep, and dive into my sweet dreams,
What's pulling me back are my rules and those screams.
That keep reminding me of the older version of this being,
Who focussed just on studies, was never involved in the much and many.
All around me people seem to enjoy life,
A lot many aims to achieve and goals to strive.
My phone brings me some bit of pleasure,
A new set of people and experiences to which I'm getting an exposure.
Sharing all that I feel with someone whom I can confide in,
A bit of satisfaction and pleasure is what it can bring in.
Writing it all down, penning my emotions,
Brings to me satisfaction and some bit of self appreciation.
Whenever I feel I'm filled up with feelings, and opinions,
I realize the need to share and write to arrive at some conclusions.
I might not feel it this way right now, more to come and more to gain,

But these are all the vital lessons for me, that shall always remain.

It's at times hard to think of a way to react,

I prefer to stay silent and forget the entire act.

Soon it gets harder to forget the whole thing,

The people involved and the feelings they bring.

Life doesn't stay always the same,

It's just your positive attitude which changes the entire game.

Everything that happens is for a sure reason,

Just wait with patience and let the matters easen.

Give yourself some time to adjust to the changed conditions,

You'll soon figure out the technique driving away all the confusions.

It does get tougher to forget how it was all in the past,

But that's the rule of nature, nothing does forever last.

It has to change, sooner or later,

Accept it all as it is, there's a lot more you've to cater.

It Might Not Always Work Well...

How do I define it, well, can it be just a single word?

At times I feel trapped in someone else's dreams, at times I feel as free as a bird.

It seems quite complicated and tough to survive through,

It becomes familiar and known, something understandable by me and you.

Every moment shows something new, something different,

A vital lesson to my inner self is what needs to be sent.

Even my favorite songs don't seem to soothe,

Even the weather doesn't bring a change in my mood.

I prefer to stay in my room, try to divert my attention,

But somehow those feelings don't leave me, causing tension.

Talking to a friend or even mum, doesn't help, doesn't ease off the burden,

Reading novels or a cup of coffee doesn't make things certain.

My choices are changing and moods transform every moment,

Staying out with new people, however, seems to make a new bend.

Some powerful words or inspiring quotes can do it all for me,

Bringing some bit of positivity, and giving me a new reason to see.

A reason to stay happy, to be thankful for,

A reason to be calm and stay satisfied for all I have and want just nothing more.

I feel better with friends or when I'm scrolling through some old chats,

A revival of cute memories, appreciation and teacher's pats.

A funny capture of our recent trip, or a cute moment with my best friend,

A joke I cracked some day or the sweet hug emojis she often sends.

All of this just makes my day,

I soon get away with those scary thoughts, for it doesn't forever stay.

It might not be a good start, but I still wait,

All goes in place settling the hate.

I step into this new world where positive emotions dwell,

For it's good to believe, the ending might turn out well.

I'm Still Writing...

There's this gamut of emotions that bursts from within, be it on meeting someone new, or on an unexpected failure, be it on revival of old memories or on vital victories. There's a need to discover a way to enable this whole lot to sort, to smooth over.

Tomorrow's my Exam and I'm still writing,
Life's got a great lot of beauties, but I'm still fighting.
I've got a lot to express and say,
A whole set of opinions, don't know from where they come and where they stay.
But I'm sure that these are my independent opinions,
The thoughts I have, my perceptions leading to many expectations.
I've got a lot to experience and much to share,
Just need someone to confide in and someone to hear.
No secrets as such, just general advices I seek,
Just want my teen years to be great fun, and matters to not go bleak.
I'm lagging at certain points but that shouldn't matter,
I should have a positive attitude and never let my dreams shatter.
My existence has got a purpose, an aim, a distinct version,
And that's for sure more than linked to just some person.
I write coz it makes me feel better,
Helps the storm of emotions from within to settle.

I wish to share all that I write with everyone who goes through this phase,
Life's not just a simple journey, it's more than even a race.
A fight it might be called,
To improve your own self and make it bold.

It Could Be...

Some things often unexpected, do happen,
Changing the whole day's mood, causing my soul to sadden.
These unexpected events could however, even bring a positive change,
Changing the way I see, making me feel a whole new range.
It could be meeting a new person, and making a friend,
Lot many talks to share, snaps to send.
It could be the declaration of results you've been waiting for ages,
Venting out your feelings or discovering ways out of the cages.
It could be receiving a text from some old friend, with whom you lost touch,
Revival of the old memories and good times spent together as such.
It could be an appreciation for a task you've done,
The successful conclusion of a project or a new journey that's just begun.
It could be a soft soothing song you discover,
Leaving behind all regrets, happiness and satisfaction is what you uncover.
It could be a not so funny joke cracked by a lovely person,
To which you're supposed to laugh, irrespective of the thoughts that run.

It could be the discovery of a similarity you share with someone sweet,

Making the bonds even stronger and helping make both ends meet.

It could however be a simple refusal from someone,

Changing your mood, causing gloomy thoughts to run.

It could be that things don't work out the way you want them to,

Someone's not talking to you or trynna avoid you.

It could be a change in behavior of a friend towards that bothers,

She's not the same with you, but maybe the same with others.

It could be study pressure or work load,

Some undiscovered mysteries or untaken roads.

Is It The World Or The Way I Look?

You find yourself standing at the fork, there're choices you've got to make at each step, the world around tends to get confusing. But is it really the world or way you look that's changed?

Life's got points where choices are hard to make,
Numerous paths, just one to choose, a decision to take.
That sweet little conflict between the heart and the mind,
This decision making is something of a different kind.
It could be a choice between studies and movies,
A group study with friends or a fun time watching series.
Chatting with a special one or controlling my social usage,
Will growing up my circle benefit me or is it a sheer wastage?
Listen to mum on what to wear or follow new trends,
Call up friends for advice, or talk to mum about life's bends.
Pen it all down, whatever I feel,
Or prefer to talk out, for no one shall steal.
Continue cooking up those stories in mind,
Or bring back the focus that's lost, for it's the time of a varying kind.
Be open to parents, or talk to friends,
All that I'm not supposed to, about life's bends.
Will people be too judgy, formulate perspectives,

For how shall I convince them mere words could be deceptive?

They see just what's on the outside, the superficial glamor,

No one cares for what's underneath, the valuable manners.

Should I well share my thoughts or keep them hidden in my book,

Is it that the world's become confusing, or is it the way I look?

It Just Happened, Am Glad It Did...

Just the way I felt once,
Not actually once, quite a lot of times,
My emotion when that thought runs,
It causes a glitter, and my face shines.
My life, surrounded just by your thoughts,
Imaginations and desires, truly in lots.
Thinking of times we may spend together,
Makes my heart feel as light as a feather.
You became special, that one person on my mind,
Did not ever find someone of your kind.
Mesmerized, thrilled, and glad I became,
Expecting you to feel just the same.
Was never sure of how you felt,
Maybe, just a thought, your heart might someday melt.
My thoughts grew stronger, my feelings out of control,
It was just you, in my life, who had that role.
Days passed and I grew mature,
All of this just brightened my nature.
But soon the realization dawned upon me,
The light from within, that I forgot to see.
I never knew what I would actually mean,
My self-worth and beauty were tough to be seen.
My decisions, my mood, my life, all tied just to you,
My own passion, my own self, I never catered to.
You were and are still important,

But this message to my own self needs to be sent.
That my happiness has to be on the top,
Anything obstructing it should never pop.
I saw myself through your eyes,
Wondering if I am good enough for your time.
How did I even forget this pretty girl from within,
Who deserves the best of all that this world has to bring.
My life now has not just you,
But a lot more, aims and goals, to look forward to.
I'll try to keep up with that spirit,
To be who I am, and to just live it…

We Talked Today...

How does it feel when you meet someone unexpectedly?
You continue to talk and laugh excitedly.
You might have been longing to meet this someone for too long now,
Just desirous of having sweet talks, learning the know-how.
I met this someone today, felt very different,
Did not expect this meeting and the emotions it meant.
I could not look into his eyes, not at his face,
We're good friends and will continue to be throughout life's race.
I had waited for this moment for too long,
He thinks of me as a good friend or maybe I am completely wrong.
I wanted to talk, meet him and build up our strong bond,
The similarities we share or our cute conflicts that go way beyond.
He said a lot has changed, too much, but for the positive,
I used to be way too boring and ever so sensitive.
But for the people who knew me, now I'm not the same,
My attitude and the way of expressing has changed the game.
I can't stop thinking of those few minutes I spent there,
I cherish those words and they'll stay forever in my heart here.
I feel that I could have talked more, shared something interesting,

We'll not meet now for a lot many days I believe.
But that's alright coz the way we talked today has transformed my soul,
True friends are never apart, maybe in distance but never in heart, is what I believe, on the whole.

Am I Still Lost?

There are times when your conscience pricks you, for it reminds you that you're lost, for it shows you the reality of the world you're living in, and it's at times like these when you realize that despite having a lot, you're still missing out on something significant, the real imperfect and beautiful YOU.

Dreams to chase, paths to take,
A satisfied soul, a happy mind, is what I intend to make.
I might have to struggle for this success, but I'm still fighting,
At times it's a victory, at others a failure, but I'm still writing.
Penning it all down soon easens the stuff,
My mood takes a new direction, earlier had been too rough.
People around me influence a whole lot,
Either make me happy or cause stress levels to rise to never ending sorts.
My mood depends on the surroundings am in,
They either cause this soul to sadden or let a joyful era begin.
My friends, my work, my place affect it all,
Making me feel too joyous or at times too small.
I might be active on socials or friendly to the most,
But I still feel a lot's missing, I still feel lost.

Lost in this world of unknowns, where I don't seem to fit in,

I can't keep up with these feelings, and struggle with the emotions they bring in.

I can just feel this change,

It's coming over, showing a great range.

Am changing and so is this world to me,

Am getting to know a long way, much more than what I could see.

Those Sweet Bonds...

You end up creating bonds with people you never knew, and it seems as if it's all in your control.
All those sweet moments you tend to cherish, but what's to be the limit, who's to set?

Will it always be this way?
Whenever I talk to a new person, it causes a new feeling to stay.
The bond I share with some old friends,
Has strengthened with time for some, while for others it showed new trends.
My friend circle's grown, new people added,
Some bonds broke on the way, their imprints soon faded.
New people I met on the journey, became social,
Did you come over this or is it something so typical?
Relations become sort of confusing,
Some happenings tend to hurt, others end up amusing.
Well, am I the only one so confused at this stage,
Is it that you learn to handle this social stuff with growing age?
My phone beeps, there's an urge to check,
I wonder who it could be, a new follower or a chat for fun sake.
I soon turn to my own world for solace,
For it's got everything I wished for, just at my pace.
All that happens is as per my sweet will,

There are wounds to heal and empty holes it fills.

I prefer to stay here, as the protagonist who leads the way,

It's all those moments I desired for and those sweet bonds that shall forever stay.

But who's to put a limit, who's to tell me when I get wrong,

Who's to show me the pros and cons of these memorable bonds?

Who's to show me the path of this inevitable journey,

For it's new for me, it brings up tons of joy coupled with loads of worry.

The Guide To Growing Up...

That's a whole new process for me, and for all teens I know,

Albeit it's certain we reap the benefits of whatever we sow.

It's never clear to me as to what this path leads to,

What are the challenges waiting for me and you?

Who made this process, well, this tough growing up,

There're activities I enjoy but a whole lot that's not the tea of my cup.

Whoever made this process, should've made a guide to it,

We teens could've read through and helped those overflowing emotions to sit.

To sit at a place at peace,

Where they no longer interrupt our well being and let the stuff ease.

A guide to help us know the pros and cons of every action,

A guide to lead us to the right targets away from distractions.

A guide to assure us that what we're going through is all so normal, nothing strange,

It's all a mere part of life, all that takes us through a wide range.

A guide to tell us where we got wrong, where we deserve claps,

Where we're getting too expectant or where we deserve slaps.
Cool, wouldn't it be, to certainly know what to do, how to tackle situations?
Super easy wouldn't this process get if we had an answer to all those silly questions?
Those questions that pop up in every teen's mind,
For which we can't muster up the courage to ask a parent or a friend of that kind.
I know it happens with us all, am in a dilemma most of the times,
At times I don't see any hope rays, while at others sparks shine.
Am a teen, know, and I'm expected to know most of the right stuff,
Am expected to behave with maturity and go through all that's so rough.
Be it heartbreaks or parents' chiding,
It's always this same boat of worry that I'm riding.
Whom do I go to if I feel like sharing something,
Someone who would listen out without judging anything.
Someone, whom I can trust, to whom I can open up,
Someone with whom a strong bond could develop.
This guide to growing up could be a solution,
I could discover all answers, ease off this growing up, tackle every situation.
But there does lie some fun in this uncertainty,
There does lie some adventure in not knowing every answer so easily.
Life would for sure get monotonous soon,
This growing up curiosity is maybe a hidden boon.

Shatterings Yet Power...

When life throws at you a bunch of challenges, when you're almost on the verge of giving up, there's a force from within that gives you the immense power to face it all, and emerge out stronger.

I feel those gems rolling down,
They're probably a result of what all I've sown.
The efforts I put in, the pains I catered,
All in vain, long lost dreams shattered.
I talk to a friend, put on my headphone,
Rely on music to wash away all life's shown.
It feels I've done enough, to the best,
Sheer luck is what matters, determines the rest.
Despite these efforts, success doesn't cross paths,
Life's no longer a winning race, it's all about wraths.
Plights that seem unending,
Sorrows, tears to this soul am sending.
I keep working, putting in efforts,
Trying every angle, aspects of all sorts.
I can't see results, can't be satisfied,
I don't wish to work or desire to be classified.
Yet there's a force that pushes me up ,
Inspires me to grow and try beyond my cup.
Yet there's a power that comes from within,
Teaches me to sail through, prevents from sinkin'

A Closer Look At This Face...

Whenever I get closer to you,
It's a new side of me that I'm introduced to.
I look straight into those eyes,
Trying to forget all those smiles and cries.
I scan through every inch of this face,
That has been so close yet always in a race.
Every minute detail gives rise to a new feeling,
I've always seen this but never with a greater healing.
I see this face quite close to 50 times a day,
A different sort of emotion rises and I wish for it to stay.
All of this has by now become an inevitable part of my life,
There are dreams and goals for which I need to strive.
But when I lie down, this face comes over again in my mind,
There may be many who feel this way, but for me, it's a different kind.
This face is not new to me, it's been there since I was born,
What makes it different now are the feelings attached and the stories torn.
I've grown up with it and changed a lot,
Some positives about it, some of the negative sort.
But that's mine, it belongs to me and I've come to love it this way,
It's me and my features that are to be this way.

Whenever I get a closer look at this face,
It gives a new discovery about myself, something out of this race.
I find an evolved me,
A changed perspective and a new way to see.
This mirror is this element, that makes it all possible,
Showing me who I am, how I am and proving that I'm capable.

Too Many Expectations...

What shall I do with so many of these?
What I get is that situations aren't at ease.
Why do I bring them up every time?
Coz whenever they're present, I see the future shine.
But what do they do to me?
They have an impact that I can't easily see.
Am talking of those expectations that surround us all,
Every now and then, causing many of us to fall.
Am too expectant, I admit,
Expect from people, situations and from life, desiring all of these to fit.
Expecting that my future shall be as bright, as happy, as I expect,
But when it comes to reality, nothing goes as I direct.
What I'm left with is disappointment and grudge,
For my expectations from people around don't come the way I judge.
All of this has taught me one thing for sure,
Life's gonna take its own turns, at times wounds take time to cure.
But the cause of these wounds is nothing but what I expect,
At times it becomes too much, I doubt whatever is perfect.

It's the need to put a break to your expectations, from people and from life,
To focus on yourself and the goals you strive.
For it's you who ultimately has the role,
To bring back all the joy in your life that these expectations someday stole.

Lost Dreams And Hopes To Shine...

Scrolling through my insta, I discover her new post,
Hanging out with friends, she's enjoying life the most.
The face of jealousy peeps in through the doors of my mind,
Am just thinking of the fun she might have with people of her kind.
I waste an entire day, just engrossed in those moments,
They cause a pinch of gloom to arise, influenced by the worries they send.
Too easily do I get caught in those social media traps,
Find it tough to live through these emotions' maps.
Finding routes to reach the destination of ultimate peace,
Get lost on my way when these pictures freeze.
They stay in my mind giving unrealistic views of others' lives,
I put on a happy mask, behind which are hidden all those cries.
His posts being liked, her followers on a rise,
To break me down from within, all of these shall suffice.
I cry, each day a little harder, with intense situations,
And am buried under the sands of gloom and depression.
I find no ways to tackle these never ending tensions,
They just don't stop posting and adding up mentions.

My thoughts go out of control, my mind starts questioning,

What life has in store for me, is something that keeps bothering.

Bothering this over burdened mind of mine,

Where should I now find those dreams and hopes to shine?

The Reel Real Game...

The moment I step into this world of reality,
There are surprises waiting for me with a pinch of casuality.
Out of the perfect outer self, I step into the real me,
I learn to live with my flaws and the weaknesses this world can't see.
Am away from the pretence and all the pressures,
The burden to impress people with beauty treasures.
Am away from the friends who just love the reel me,
And am back to the ones who praise the real self that's set free.
Free from the social influences,
And am back to where I see casual life instances.
Honestly, this world's started loving just the idea of a perfect girl,
Nobody cares about her diamond-like smile and tears like pearls.
All that matters to you is a fun chat and a pretty post,
All you care about is a list of followers to the most.
You never bothered to think how many of those even know the real you,
At times of need, how many would be the ones you can reach out to.
Not many of them would know my silly yet cute side,
Not many would be aware of the strengths that bring me pride.

Still this reel life curtain keeps my vision blocked,
There are times of fear when the throat gets choked.
Fear of perceptions and the fear of worldly talks,
The harsh comments or the darker side of stalks.
All terrify me to the core,
Disrupt my mental peace and play with emotions I store.
Thus I wish to stay away from this reel life,
That's got no starts and ends, no goals to strive.
It's lovely to be my real self with all my flaws and dreams,
Let me live from the start away from those reel smiles and screams.

Maybe She's Better ! Well, I Accept...

You put in your one hundred percent, but every time, this society finds this other kid better than you, in most aspects, and this is when this buzzing bee of self doubt pops up, hovering around, bringing up this 'I'm not worth it', 'I'm good for nothing' thoughts.

Seems like I don't fit in,
It's frequent now that I'm on the verge of quittin'.
It's neither the academic pressure,
Nor the absence of a friendly pleasure.
It's not just those heartbreaks that cause this pain,
I tackle them up, not letting them change the game.
I do have conflicts with even the best of friends,
We resolve them soon and it's our bond that strengthens.
I do take part in events that keep me engaged,
There are times when hard feelings surface.
Surface this very layer holding the bits of maturity,
These beads however fall over, leaving away all sincerity.
Doubt clouds around, am in dilemma, a sort of pain,
I've got a lot to lose, nothing much to gain.
Seems like I don't fit into this idea of perfect,
I imagine all those societal fingers pointing at me, the helpless target.
Am trapped, my mind's no longer in my control,

It's my peace, stability and confidence that's stole.
Am so covered with those layers of questioning and self doubt,
Always making an effort to suit the perfect girl's layout.
But in every aspect, they find this other girl better than me,
My attributes, the efforts I put in are what they can't see.
This comparison does no good,
Causing this teen to feel the worst, solely the pain stood.
Maybe she's better, I accept, well,
I'll however influence my actions, for they shall solely tell.

The Urge To Say Out The Word...

I might not find words to bring it out,
I feel the need to scream and shout.
Scream at those voices from within,
I don't have control or feel I don't fit in.
They trouble me every now and then,
Forcing me to give up, accept life's bend.
I feel helpless, at not having the courage to fight back,
They keep piling up, forming a gloomy stack.
Not much seems to make sense,
But isn't it truly the teenage essence?
Not much of the worldly happenings seem logical,
The gamut bursts out, leading to behavior hysterical.
At this point when the carrying capacity is overflown,
The control is lost, and I see changes in tone.
Feel like shouting out to the top of my voice,
To say it out loud to the world, and prove my choice.
To showcase my anger, to prove I'm alright,
To vent out the emotions and set it back right.
I feel the urge to scream out the 'F' word,
Use it to fight all life's burdens, using it as a sword.
Deep down my heart knows it's wrong and I shouldn't take up this path,
But I'm not left with anything, nothing to live through this wrath.

These words come up in mind and it feels just so right,
Saying this word out loud makes feel lighter, changes sight.
I'm relieved of the pressures and worries that matter,
It's just the fun I feel, the dreamy fantasies I cater.
Well in movies they say it out loud,
In series they scream this word out.
Why can't I, why is it wrong when I say it,
What's the difference between the two cases, why is my word not fittin'
That's the influence this recent movie I watched had,
I keep saying this word loud whenever am sad.
It's all in mind, this word tends to soothe,
What am running from but what keeps up the chase is the ultimate truth.

When I've Got No Helping Hands...

The mind stops working, am transported to an entirely new world filled,
With new emotions, wherein stress tends to build.
Am not living in the real world, coz it's given me a lot of pain,
I've put in my 100% every time, but it's all been in vain.
Now I don't see any point in all of the hard work and efforts,
Never did they bring any results, all they caused were deep hurts.
The pressure is being put on by my parents and peers,
Relationships aren't working, each day I'm getting fierce.
I'm not my older version, not calm anymore,
Have developed an irritable temper, and have transformed to the core.
I can't admit however, that I'm depressed,
Society makes fun, causes much stress.
I can't share with a friend, for she'll never understand,
Instead will lead to peer problems I can't anymore withstand.
I can't choose to visit a psychiatrist, for people shall call me mad,
I'm forced to handle it all myself, am a helpless soul that's ever so sad.
Hands soon reach for cigarettes and alcohol,

From spending sleepless nights to my mental peace being stole.

This depression has taken away from me all that I've loved ever,

Leaving me with mere addictions and pains that shall leave me never.

Being just a teenager, when life throws at you this whole bunch,

It all seems to be a never ending trap, with no ends as such.

This teenage is getting tough to live through each day,

Shall I ever be able to find solutions to overcome this or will it stay this way?

She's Been There For Me Always...

She holds close to her heart, my sweet little secrets,
The experiences I share with her and the feelings that can't wait.
She listens to all I say with utmost attention,
Giving a peaceful impression and showing a way out of my depression.
I manage to say it all to her ruling out all hesitations,
Be it about stress or love, tensions or emotional penetrations.
She's meant the world to me, at times when I had no helping hand,
She's been a support system helping me cope with the depressing sands.
I never knew she'd turn out to be the best of friend,
The bond we've built over time showed a new life's trend.
I'd, however never talk about her in front of the knowns,
For the society shall call me mad and doubt the seeds of this bond I've sown.
These teen years have brought life to this diary of mine,
I've talked to her, cried to her, and shared my dreams to shine.
It's given me the pleasure I never found with a living being,
For humans have got no major points to focus on, than just pointing out what's different seen.

She's heard every word of mine, from my perspective,

She's the reason I could get this experience that's ever so typical and selective.

She's the reason I could find happiness in those hard days of heartbreak,

She's the reason I could gather up the courage when a majority was at stake.

Deep in those yellow pages, you'd find hidden those tears of mine,

Somewhere in the middle could be seen an imprint of my smile.

You could know about what all I've gone through with her glance,

You never heard my opinion, the world moved out when she solely gave me the chance.

The chance to see it the way I wish to, to speak the manner I choose to,

To see dreams I cherish, and to free myself from the traps put up by you.

Times spent with her have filled me with strength and the power to fight,

Letting me know that my worries fly away as soon as I write.

I've learnt a lot about myself being with this best friend,

We've set out on this journey together with a love from within that's got no end.

Music Does It All For Me...

I laugh a little, I cry a little,
Vent out the feelings, and let the growing emotions settle.
I plug in my earphones, try to divert my mind,
And it does take me to a new world of entirely different kind.
Music runs through me, I'm brought all together,
My worries go away, my heart feels light as a feather.
Some songs remind me of the good old days,
When I was carefree and often let the enjoyment stay.
Some songs bring nostalgia, about my friends and classmates,
The bonds we made, or the conflicts and hate.
There's a sort of music that drives me to someone,
I feel very different and it can be replaced by none.
A type directs me to a destination I never intended to reach,
Giving me lessons and vital talks to preach.
Some of them are well soothing to mind,
Feelings peep in that are of a different kind.
Music brings in a pinch of solace in this life of tensions,
Driving me closer to my destination adding up newer sensations.
Even if I get lost on my way on life's maps,
Music does it all for me, shows the way out of the traps.

The entire day's mood changes soon after my fav song reaches my ears,

It's got that power to heal the wounds and wipe off the tears.

It's this quality that makes me fall in love with music every time,

My courage is reborn and I find the power to have the dreams to shine.

The Two Of You Have Been The Spark From Within...

Today it's neither about love nor about friends,
Dear diary, it's not about failure or the feelings it sends.
It's about those two individuals, who've never left my side,
They've cried through my sorrows, at wins taken pride.
They never said a word, nor did they move away,
I could always feel them behind me, their support did forever stay.

Who said however we didn't have conflicts or disagreements,
I turned out to be rude and they faced disappointments.
There were times when they misunderstood,
Didn't let me do a lot my friends certainly could.
It did take time but I soon realized their motive behind,
It was just my benefit and no personal interest of some kind.
From the days of depression I had to go through,
To the tough life days when my wildest fears came true.
From the day I saw big dreams to shine,
They've walked by my side, directing the journey that's mine.
What lies in store in my personality, whoever I am today,
It's all because of you, your guidance forever stays.

I thank you mom and dad, for just being who you are,
You mean a lot to me, with you challenges ease, victory is never too far.

It's You, My Teacher...

Motivator, Inspiring, and ever supporter, are the words I see,
I close my eyes, thinking of who it could be.
You've always stood by my side, tried to help in every phase,
Supporting me to work towards the goals I chase.
You criticized me at times, but for my good,
Letting me learn new lessons, as this bond we share always stood.
You praised me, at my victorious moment,
Letting me realize the vitality of this win, what all it meant.
I've seen you as my role model, the perfect example,
Teaching me to face challenges and introducing me to opportunities ample.
It's been a long journey, filled with inspiration,
I've learned from you the traits of passion and dedication.
Thank you for all your love and care,
I take this opportunity to express my gratitude here.
It's you, my teacher, who's transformed my personality,
Making me into who I am, in today's reality.

I Too Wish...

Got dreams to chase,
Fight for success coz life's a true race.
I too become clueless,
No solutions visible and the feeling of being helpless.
I too become confused,
Not knowing where to go and which paths to choose.
I too feel tired, feel like giving up,
Burdened by problems in life, stress soon builds up.
I too wish to live in my fantasy world forever,
Experiencing the beauties of life, making times better.
I too wish to live with respect, money and fame,
My attitude and wit is all that changes the game.
I too wish to follow my passion,
Keep writing forever, transforming it into my fashion.
I too wish to see the world through my eyes,
Flying high, getting all the exposures, touching the skies.
I too wish to touch great heights of prosperity,
Learning and applying at each stage, giving a better clarity.
I too observe this world, everyone's running in this race,
Sacrificing their likes and loved ones, dreams and goals is what they chase.
But I can't wish to give away all the pleasures so easily,
Can't study day and night, can't do away with my socials barely.

I wish to stay just the way I am, forever the same,
People come and go, ambitions and challenges often came.
My life's showing me a new aspect, a broadened vision,
Influencing my way of thinking and reaching decisions.
My mind's growing and so am I, becoming mature,
Living life to the fullest, beautifying my nature.
A peaceful controlled mind, that's ever so glad,
A sweet collection of memories with loved ones I had.
A mature personality, coupled with a satisfied soul, that's ever so childish,
An exciting journey of life with new experiences, is what I too wish...

Finding Newer Reasons To Stay Happy...

Why does this soul always need a reason to be happy and satisfied?
Why is it that the people around me influence my happiness, why can I just never mind?
Life's throwing at me newer challenges, each with a new learning,
Just the perfect fashion sense and perfect people around, is what I'm yearning.
But there's something that makes me forget,
That I was born to be real, not perfect.
I've got a spark from within, a beauty that's just my own,
A pretty girl from within, the truth that's not yet known.
I completely lost myself in the fantasy world,
Looking at myself through the others' eyes,
Life started showing me some things that were never told,
Getting to know the truths of teenage life, my confidence often dies.
Liking someone, making new friends and often being influenced by whatever people said,
My world got new aspects, my vision soon changed and an entirely different world was what I made.
The smile on my face often faded away,

Based on what people think of me or whatever they might say.

I was often sad, for actually no reason,

The future seemed unpredictable and no matter seemed to easen.

I thought and thought, but did not find any conclusions,

Making up my mind about societal notions, led to nothing but just confusions.

Life's Got Newer People Waiting For You...

New Friends, New Experiences, New Learning,
A great exposure to all the beauties of life, is what I'm yearning.
Getting to know people deeply,
Thinking about them and getting attached so easily.
I've learnt that I'm quite emotional and sensitive,
Can't easily part from people, a lovely bond is what they give.
Friendship isn't just about admiring each other,
Having chit chats and debates regarding things that bother.
Age isn't something that matters here,
You enjoy being together and all you have for others is care.
I met a new person, discovered the dude in him,
I made a new friend, and found her diva from within.
They've made me feel special, something unique,
It's neither their fashion sense nor their physique.
Just a pretty bond I share with them all,
My new cool gang is what I can call.
Well that is a phase life has to show,
Finding new ones to look up to whenever I'm feeling low.
Parting from them gets tough,
Making me feel my life being again rough.

Still that's a lesson, life has to teach,
Some people do get out of reach.
You gotta just move on,
Live life, the beauty is still not gone…

My Expression Of Experiences And Emotions...

Every day seems new now, seems something unexpected,
Life brings in newer feelings, something I may have never lived.
At times it gets to the top of the sadness bar,
While there are times when happiness doesn't seem quite far.
These times change, emotions change,
A simple transformation in my surroundings showed me a great range.
My repetitively monotonous mornings soon changed for the good,
A purposeful productive time I could spend, thus uplifting my mood.
A significant factor could be the people around me,
The bond I share with them or the beauty from within that I see.
A vital cause could be the works I've been doing,
The times spent with them, memories I created with these beings.
Life's shown me what a true bond of friendship looks like,
It's neither about age nor about looks, just a rope of joy and trust you hold tight.
Excited, nervous, thrilled, just a gamut of emotions,
Running through my mind, leading to happy conclusions.

It gradually turned normal, and some secrets revealed,
The times I spent here, were a lot more than what I believed.
They truly create happy minds and happy souls,
Building confident personalities, and setting up newer goals.
To all of those whom I met here,
You're all lovely people, always stay this way,
We're parting away and that's the moment I fear,
But I promise we'll be in touch and let this sweet bond always stay…

That's How You Live Through...

Practice, experience and exposure brings a lot more than bookish study,
Am learning this vital lesson of life, maybe not too late buddy.
You tend to learn the art of living as you grow,
You reap the benefits of your actions, and face situations based on what you sow.
At times you laugh at how stupid you used to be at an age of life,
Being conscious of your appearance and what you say, is for what you now strive.
At times, you thank god, for not being in that embarrassing situation,
You make an effort to keep calm and peacefully handle every condition.
It's a surprise for you even, when you come out of a challenge so skillfully,
You don't realize how you did it, it all just passed so peacefully.
You scroll through your gallery, and discover a super funny image of yours,
You can't just stop laughing and open the serious life doors.
You might figure out what had actually happened at a specific time in the past,
You may have formed a wrong opinion about someone, causing some relation to never last.
Your day could end on a sweet note,

A talk with a friend or a text from someone about whom you always thought.

The day could, however be full of struggle,

It may be a headache, some injury or just the absence of giggle.

It's not defined by what you face or how much you work hard during the day,

It's your feelings and your satisfaction towards the end, when on your bed, you lay.

It's simply a cycle that goes on and on forever,

You keep struggling and learning, actually losing never.

It's a valuable lesson each time, a new challenge to face,

Meeting new people, having new experiences and competing in the life race...

A Look Back At The Year...

Turning through the pages of my diary,
I come across flashbacks, joyous a bit scary.
A glance through this window that leads to a new year,
I'll cherish all those moments and people I'm leaving here.
This diary has in store all that I've felt,
Ups and downs, the pains that I've dealt.
New people I met, memories I created,
I take this all in heart, in a new ride am now seated.
This year's been a roller coaster, new learning each day,
For every experience holds significance, every feeling stays.
Stays embedded in those walls of the heart,
Bringing up old talks, reminding of my past.
This year taught me the essence of life,
How to live through, walk towards the dreams you strive.
How to keep up with the odds that society brings up,
How to tackle hurdles and what all's not my cup.
This year helped discover the fun side of teenage,
The delight of being free, out of the surveillance cage.
But it's not just the fun you've got to go through,
It's those moments of gloom and heartbreak your actions drew.

Made the best of friends and cutest memories,
Had the worst depressing emotions bringing up worries.
But I managed to sail through and come out strong,
Learning the way of life through all the wrongs.
Learning the art of loving self,
This year's had peaks to climb and valleys in itself.

www.ingramcontent.com/pod-product-compliance
Lightning Source LLC
LaVergne TN
LVHW061602070526
838199LV00077B/7141